If you were me and lived in...
SOUTH KOREA

A Child's Introduction to Cultures Around the World

Carole P. Roman

To the girls at Diva- Your warm welcome and graciousness is an inspiration and a reflection of the land of your birth.

ISBN: 1481062344

ISBN 13: 9781481062343

Library of Congress Control Number: 2012922236

CreateSpace Independent Publishing Platform, North Charleston, SC

SEOUL

SOUTH KOREA

If you were me and lived in South Korea, your home would be in East Asia, somewhere here.

2

You might live in the capital city, Seoul. It is the largest city in South Korea and was built on the banks of the Han River. People have lived there for over two thousand years.

Your name could be Minjoon, Jihoo, or Minjae if you are a boy, and Soobin, Jiwoo, or Yeeun if you are a girl.

When you buy toys, you would pay with a won, which is like a dollar bill.

If a friend came to visit, you would surely go to Min Sok Chon, the Korean Folk Village and museum in the city of Yongin-si. It is a village of homes, markets, and workshops that show what Korean life was like five hundred years ago. There is an amusement park and lots of traditional shows depicting music and dancing.

Then you would take your friend to eat in one of the restaurants, where you would have bulgogi, or Korean barbeque. They would cook the meat right at the table on a very hot plate. You would love to eat it with kimchee, which is fermented cabbage and can be spicy. Rice is usually always on the table. You would eat your meal with metal chopsticks.

Taekwondo is an ancient martial art of self-defense. It is a wonderful way to exercise and might be your favorite sport. Of course, your little sister might like playing with her agi inhyeong, or baby doll.

The Lunar New Year is called Seol-nal and would probably be your favorite holiday. You would dress in traditional clothes called hanbok. You would visit with family and enjoy a festive dinner of soup with rice cakes.

You would be proud when you visited your grandparents and bow deeply to them with respect. You would say, "Have a blessed New Year," and they would reward you with crisp paper money in a beautiful and colorful envelope.

When you go to school, you would call it haggyo.

So now you see, if you were me, how life in South Korea could really be.

24

Pronunciation

Seoul (S-oh-l)

Minjoon (min-joon)

Jihoo (Gee-ho)

Minjae (Min-ja-ee)

Soobin (Soo-been)

Jiwoo (Ge-woo)

Yeeun (ee-yoon)

Won-(one)

Omma (O-ma)

Appa (A-Pa)

Min Sok Chon (Mien-so-chun)

Youngin-si (Yon-gin-see)

Bulgogi (bul-go gee)

Kimchee (kim-chee)

Taekwando (Tay-Quon-doe)

Agi Inhyeaong (ah-gee in-hi-yon)

Seol-nal (S-oh-nal)

Hanbok (han-bow)

Haggya (hag-yee-oh)